*Postcards*

"I love that works of art are printed so anyone can buy them. The variety of what they put on little postcards astounds me."

~ Leonard Lauder

## Also by Ben Nuttall-Smith

Blood, Feathers and Holy Men – Historical Novel (Libros Libertad 2011)

Secrets Kept / Secrets Told – Novel/Memoir (Libros Libertad 2012)

Henry Hamster Esquire – an illustrated story for children. (Nuttall-Smith 2012)

Grandpa's Homestead – Haiku for children of all ages, illustrated by Jan Albertin. (Nuttall-Smith 2012)

A Moment In Eternity (Silver Bow Publishing 2013)

# Postcards

## Ben Nuttall-Smith

Silver Bow Publishing
720 – 6th Street, Box #5
New Westminster, BC
V3L 3C5 CANADA

Copyright © 2013 Silver Bow Publishing
Cover Photo/Painting: Ben Nuttall-Smith
Cover Design: Janet Kvammen
Layout & Design: Candice James
Editing: Candice James

All rights reserved including the right to reproduce or translate this book or any portions thereof, in any form

Library and Archives Canada Cataloguing in Publication

First Edition

ISBN 978-1-927616-03-1

silverbowpublishing@gmail.com
© 2013 Silver Bow Publishing
ISBN 978-1-927616-03-1

Silver Bow Publishing
Box 5 - 720 Sixth St.,
New Westminster, BC
V3L 3C5 CANADA
Email: silverbowpublishing@gmail.com

Website: http://silverbowpublishing.shawwebspace.ca

Online Store http://www.alibris.com/stores/silverbow/

# Contents

## Ireland / 9
Belfast – Northern Ireland
Derry / Londonderry
The Antrim Coast
Foive Stitches
The Soccer Player
Irish Graveyard
Donegal (Haiku)
Dressing You Irish
Cong
Galway Roads
Ireland's Wet West Coast
Pub talk
Molly McGuiness On The Bus

## Cornwall, England / 21
Port Isaac in the Rain
Smugglers' Tunnels in Port Isaac
The Lizard
The Bofors Gun
Cadgwith Fog

## Turkey / 27
The Spice Market
Sultanahmet
Istanbul Prayer
Hagia Sophia
Grand Bazaar
House of the Blessed Virgin Mary
Tea (Çay)
Raki
Dalyan Rock Tombs
The Tour Guide
Butterfly Cove
The Hamam
Fethiye Morning
Fethiye Bay

Night Before Sailing
Early Morning in Port
Contemplating the Rocky Coast
Kekova Bay
Kale and Simena
Merchants of Kas
Café in Kas
Kas to Antalya by Dolmus
The Carpet Seller
The Carpet Weaver
Aspendos Theatre
Perge, Astendos, and Side
Kapadokya
Turkiye
Hoscakal

## Greece / 47
A Portrait Unpainted – Naoussa, Paros
Sands and Rocks (overlooking the Aegean Sea)
Swimming in the Aegean Sea
A Culinary Curiosity
Winds Across the Bay
Swimmers
All Is One
Naoussa Rocks: A Weather Report
It's All Greek to Me
A Simple Rainstorm
Yin and Yang
Peace Comes Dropping Slow
Impossible Achievements (Athens)
The Con Artist

## Italy / 59
Piazza San Marco, Venice
Puccini
The Parade of Life
The Sacred and the Profane
Venice Gliding
The Cathedral

Sunday in Florence
Past and Present: A Meditation
Smoke and Rain
Cathedral San Martino
So Little Time
Some Rain and Good Food
Florence: Beauty and Bathrooms
Le Cinque Terra
Arrividerci Roma
Sorrento
Sorrento Evening
Sorrento Haiku
Menu
The People of Capri
Victorrio
A Cure for Vertigo
Naples

## South America / 79
### Rio De Janeiro
A Samba Party
Copa Cabana Beach
### Buenos Aires
Buenos Aires in November
Ode To The Cementerio Recoleta
Plaza Dorrego
Manuella

## Mexico / 87
### Mayan Peninsula
White Sands
My Heart Is Full
Tiptoe Eyes
Of Daydreams and Seaweed
### Oaxaca City
Oaxaca weaver
Chiclets
The Zocalo
Quétzalcoatl
Of Bones

**La Manzanilla**
Carmelita's Garden
Footprints
Steet Sweeper
Señora de la gota – Bead Lady
Sunset Shift at Café de Flores
Dog in the Heat of Day
Heartbreak Melody
Dust
Pelican
Drummer
Adios

**Hawaii / 103**
Moonscape
Reading at the Beach
Kahalu'u Beach
Afternoon Beneath a Parasol

**Sunshine Coast of British Columbia / 107**
Madeira Park Palette
A Day Cruise on the Eagle
Princess Louisa Inlet
A Boat Called "Eagle"
Chatterbox Falls
Flying the Skookumchuck
Egmont Bay

**Cuba / 113**
Varadero Beach

**Poet Profile / 116**

**Ireland**

## Belfast – Northern Ireland

You have taught your sons and daughters to hate,
painted despair on thirty-foot walls,
piled loathing on fear, on ignorance, on grief.

Your children despise an enemy they do not know
while you celebrate ancient wounds, unresolved injustices,
unable to reach a fragment of truth
beyond the calumnies
you call honour, patriotism, divine right.

Weep for your children. They follow in your shame:
Falls Road, Shankill, Ulster.

While "heroes" bleed, there is no Peace.

## Derry / Londonderry

You've built a bridge, the way to Peace,
silver strand across the River Foyle,
with Music as a gift to every child
no matter creed nor parentage nor means.

With newfound hope and will,
the way is found.

The Antrim Coast

From the high pathway,
we gaze through wind-blown rain
to Rathlin and the Mull of Kintyre.
The Scottish Isles lay swathed in mist.

Some dare the swinging rope bridge at Carrick-a-Rede.
I hold my hat against the chilly gusts but do not cross.
The view is all I need.

## Foive Stitches

"Foive stitches? Foive stitches? Fer the love of Jaysus, how do ye get to have foive stitches?"

"Ta close the gap in the top o' me head."

"On the top o' th' head? Jaysus, Mary, and Joseph. an' what were ye doin' to get a gap on yer head, pray tell?"

"I were havin' a discussion wi' Mikey."

"Mike Murphy? he did this to ye? Wait till I get me hands on that little shite."

"It's all right, Ma. Mikey's my friend. He got eight."

"Eight? Eight stitches?"

"Aye. And a broken nose."

"Broken nose? Fer the love of Jaysus, was it an argument you were havin'?"

"Just a discussion, Ma."

"Just a discussion? Come here, me little lamb. Let me have a look at ye."

## The Soccer Player

"C'mon Bobby. Catch the ball. Way to go!  Good boy! "

"Now, run!  Kick it, Bobby.  Don't hold on to it.  Kick it here!"
"Don't lose it Bobby.  Kick!  Kick!"

 "Pick it up, bobby.  Oh, you butterfingers.  Kick it!"

"Dear God in heaven!  This can't be me own son."

"Ya missed it.   He missed the bloody ball!"

"C'mon Bobby. Run!  Run!  My God!  He's sitting down!"

"I don't believe it. I don't bloody believe it.    Yer sister could do better than that!"

"Get up!  Get up Bobby!  Get that bloody ball!"


"Ah!  *lay off him, Da. The lad's only four.*"

## Irish Graveyard

in life they loved, quarreled, toiled,
celebrated brief moments of joy.
now they all lie down, side by side,
waiting for the trumpet blast.
husbands, wives, lovers, children, babes.
folded hands, rosaries clasped, braided hair.
and up above, the falling leaves –
nature slowly joins them in death before rebirth.
will they hear me if i sing Danny Boy –
though soft i tread above them?

## Donegal  (Haiku)

Sheep graze in the mist
on purple hills of heather
by winding rivers.

Sun shines through the clouds
in the distance, green and gold
flicker past the lake.

From the fern-clad cliff,
sparkling, tumbling waterfalls
far beneath the bridge.

Dressing You Irish

Were I endowed with power to give
whatever you may wish,
I'd weave you a robe of emerald green
with sash of gold and blue.
All the stars would sparkle your hair
and roses red your lips.

You'd be dressed like Ireland in Summer.

## Cong

There was standing room only in Danagher's Pub
where the Guinness flowed frothy and brown.
Twenty-two rugged travelers, elbows to arse
with barely a place to put down.

The music was Irish and people joined in
one verse from an old Aussie song.
Two guitars, a squeeze box, an old Irish flute
and the rat-a-tat-tat of a drum.

## Galway Roads

beech trees
overhang sun-mottled puddles
glistening
from the night's rain
blackthorn
fringes line high hedges
freckled
with white wild garlic and bluebells

hairpin turns
spring upon narrow stone bridges
sometimes we stop and turn back
sometimes they do

sign at blind corner

free range children
careful

## Ireland's Wet West Coast

Here, on the west coast of Ireland,
man's historic melancholy
not-so-neatly segues to nature's momentous violence.
Gale force winds
whip sleet on unsuspecting travelers.
The furious ocean
sends towering waves
up miles and miles of uninhabited shorelines.
Green fields end where sandy hillocks begin,
with trees blown humpbacked by the wind.
Cliffs run ragged,
exhausted by the elements.
High hills,
like giant boulders,
slice the skyline.

I dash for shelter to jettison the wet white
from my hat and backpack.
A few minutes later,
I venture out again,
glad of a warm jacket, wool cap, and gloves.
I pass a schoolyard.
Tiny tots flap about in circles,
baby chicks in oversize parkas.
By the river, trees bend bravely in the wind.
Boats strain their moorings,
moving upstream as far as ropes allow.
While ever darker clouds forbid the sun,
church bells toll the hour.

The sun bursts out to dispel the clouds.
Surrounded by stone walls,
fields support sheep and cattle.
On front lawns, newborn lambs suckle
while older ones graze close by.
With crowds of daisies, primroses,
bluebells, and daffodils,

the fields bustle with colour.
Majestic palms are as ubiquitous as gorse,
that attractive, yellow-flowered wild bush
with an unattractive name.

Homes sport pleasant hues of yellow, blue,
and – occasionally – pink.
The traffic-congested towns look scrubbed.
Signs direct travelers
in English, Irish, and, sometimes, French.
People greet strangers.

Roofless shells of abandoned cottages
rest in fields and by roadsides,
sad reminders of sufferings long past.
Sometimes just a few stones still stand
to memorialize the monasteries and convents
laid waste by Cromwell's thugs.

## Pub Talk

"Are you from away?"
    "Yes, Canada."

"American?"
    "No, Canadian."

"Ah, what part?"
    "Vancouver."

"Vancouver. Is that near Bar Harbour, Maine? Knew a feller from Bar Harbour, Maine. Writing advertising jingles, he was."
    "Vancouver is in Canada, on the Pacific coast... Maine is northeastern United States."

"I'd love to visit Bar Harbour one of these years. Heard it's just like Ireland."
    "Ireland's a beautiful country."

"You like it here?"
    "Very nice."

"Yes, I'd really like to see Bar Harbour. Vancouver, you say."
    "Yes."

"Well, have a good holiday."
    "Thank you."

## Molly McGuiness On The Bus

An elderly lady gets on the bus
with two shopping bags.
A wayward strand of hair
falls across her brow
from beneath a bright yellow head scarf.

Huffing and puffing,
she places her packages on the top step
and grabs the side railing
as she pulls herself laboriously aboard.


The driver greets her.
"Bring yourself in out of the weather, now."

  "Oh, it's a wet one."

"'Tis at that. and yourself with no umbrella!"

  "Lost it in the wind, I did."

"Get to your seat now, before I start the bus. Mind your step."

She picks up her bags,
then grunts and farts
as she settles into the seat behind me.

Within seconds,
she strikes up a conversation with a man,
the owner of a raspy, tobacco-stained voice:

  "Away early today, Mr. Flanagan?

"Aye."... "In for a bit of shopping, were ye?"

  "A few... Would you believe who I bumped into, coming out
of O'Ryan's? Herself. Molly McGuiness. She'd not been
wastin' her afternoon. And here it was not yet four."

"Had a few, had she?"

"More than likely. I could tell you a thing or two."

"Oh, she's a nice enough person."
"When you look past her faults."

"Will you be to bingo, Thursday?"
"Perhaps."

**Cornwall**

**England**

## Port Isaac in the Rain

Today we traced the muddy path
above Port Isaac Bay,
through buttercups and daisy fields
where sheep and cattle graze,
midst scurvy grass and golden gorse
with rain clouds on the hill.
The chill wind blew with all her might
yet we continued still.

Along the cliffs the seagulls soared
above the frothy waves.
I paused to ponder pirate lore
and deep mysterious caves,
where Barbary brigands hid their gold
and hapless Cornish slaves
stood bound in chains, before the tide
swept them to watery graves.

And then we strolled through narrow lanes
with whitewashed stones and circled panes,
midst fishing nets and floats and traps
and cozy windows draped with cats.
The smoke from chimney topss curled high
above the slate roofs to the sky.

At last we sheltered from the storm
to drink and chat, all cozy warm.

*\*Partially penned in the Golden Lion beside a glowing fire.*

## Smugglers' Tunnels in Port Isaac

Beneath the chapel on Roscarrock Hill,
an ancient tunnel lies,
where rum and brandy, silk and spice
were slipped 'neath taxmen's eyes.

Those Methodists were men of God;
their hymns were loud and clear.
So sounds of contraband below
were smothered by their prayer.

While smugglers ran from ship to shore
up to the village inn,
the parson, from his pulpit, spoke
the fearful price of sin.

He railed of evil's mighty grip,
the bonds of demon rum,
and fiery paths beneath the earth
where Satan's minions run.

The just man goes to heaven
where he'll forever dwell,
whilst those who deal in contraband
end up as politicians. *(Which suits them very well.)*

## The Lizard
*\*The Lizard is the southernmost tip of England.*

windblown meadows
gully paths
great expanse of turquoise blue
boulders perched on jutted rock
crags and cliffs of rainbow hue
carpets spread in richest pink,
        serpentine with moss of gold

had I the art to paint this scene,
        I could not, were I so bold

## The Bofors Gun*

Within the shade of the Golden Lion
a rusty cannon stands:
a bofors gun from a merchant ship,
gone down with all her hands.

The valiant SS Milly
had run her final race
just two months short of Armistice
and five miles from this place.

So now she stands her lonely watch,
her sights upon the bay,
still searching for the submarine
from that bleak September day.

Her spirit fires at u-boats
and all the Kaiser's men.
A ghost upon the harbour wall,
this mighty bofors gun.

*Taken from the British Liberty Ship – S.S. Milly,
 Torpedoed five miles from Port Isaac –  September 1918.


## Cadgwith Fog

Swallows and gulls
swoop, twirl, and glide
through the field of thick white mist,
like myriad players in a sky ball game.

Beneath the field,
all framed in mottled green,
stand cottage roofs of slate and thatch.

On the hill behind, a lonely spire
invokes the sun, to break the seal of fog
and post the winning score.

# Turkey

## The Spice Market

The masses surge through the halls
– five thousand, ten, maybe more –
communing in crowded alleyways.
Eager merchants cry their wares.
They greet and smile, all polite,
to help each pilgrim find ecstasy
in nuts, figs, dates, exotic seeds,
and lentil soup, with bread and lemon slice.

The best we save for last:
Turkish delight,
in mouthwatering varieties.

At a mosque nearby,
the faithful cleanse their hands, heads, arms, feet,
in preparation for noon prayer.
Then, shoes in hand,
they prostrate themselves,
to face Quiblah.

*Qiblah also known as qibla or qiblat, is the direction for Muslims to pray. The direction is calculated for the shortest distance to the Ka'bah using the great circle.

## Sultanahmet

Their shoes in white bags,
the massed pilgrims, believer and infidel,
stand hushed,
united in awe.

Sunlight animates the stained-glass geometry
over the immense grandeur of blue-tiled walls.
Acres of carpet mark the place of prayer.

## Istanbul Prayer

Lights tease the Marmara
as the orange globe
rides an evening carpet into the sea.
From gold-lit minarets,
plaintive calls to prayer
oscillate above the city din.
And gulls float like moths
between the flaméd peaks.

## Hagia Sophia

Oh, poor lady,
robed in orange-rose and grey,
dusty and forlorn on your hill above the Marmara:
so proud you were at your birth,
by Constantine,
now so barren,
so cold,
bereft of jewels.

Cats and birds
announce your empty dome.

Yet, from beneath your blistered shell,
your former glory hints to me,
in winks and whispers.

## Grand Bazaar

The smiling merchants offer tea:
hot apple tea in small glasses
with a lump of sugar.
We examine old silver,
hand-crafted tiles,
woven silk, kilim bags,
camel bone boxes hand painted,
and perfume bottles, all exquisite.

Then we bargain, pazarlik.
Happy customer.
Happy merchant.

*kilim – a flat woven rug or carpet material.*
*pazarik – bargaining*


## House of the Blessed Virgin Mary

I walk in awe,
the rocky paths,
where John and Paul and early pilgrims
framed the Living Church.

I walk in awe,
the selfsame ground,
the Blessed Virgin once strolled.
Unheralded, this sacred hill
marks the site near Ephesus
of Mother Mary's home.

A gentle chapel now stands in the rain:
so far from Nazareth,
so far from Calvary's pain.

## Tea (Çay)

In Turkey there's a custom,
warm and friendly, come what may:
A glass of tea with sugar, offered free,
while browsing in the marketplace
or waiting in the shade
for a bus or a boat ride on the sea.

It's a brand of hospitality
the world could well adopt.
Wherever there's a stranger at the door,
serve a simple glass of apple tea
with sugar on the side.
Sit as friends
and never go to war.

## Raki

Raki is a pleasant drink.
for sharing with new friends
as we lounge by the river in the sun.
We sip Raki after dining,
with the moon bright on the bay,
while the muezzin calls the faithful to night prayer.

## Dalyan Rock Tombs

Hewn into rocky cliffs,
the tombs of kings stand empty,
their Lycean guests all fled,
expelled by thieves and tumbled from their niche.
The ravages of time have pierced their pillars.
Yet still, their beauty is magnificent to see.

We navigate blue waters far below.
And contemplating the wonders men have made,
we marvel at the skills of long ago.

## The Tour Guide

This rugged Turkish land is softened
by olive, fig, and mandarin.
On every hill and valley green,
the stones of ages past
stand row on row.
Smiling voices greet us as we walk
these paths of history.

Our guide tells stories
of each jewel, of place and sacred site,
where princes, kings, and sultans
won the land for Islam and for peace.
This happy **"Çigdem"** shares her hopes,
while her faith and history
spread like a carpet in the dazzling sun.

***Çigdem was the name of our tour guide.**

## Butterfly Cove

Near lofty, cloud-held peaks and mystery caves,
the sparkling ocean froths upon the beach,
where campers' tents sit perched amidst the trees.
We ride the swell and eat our noonday meal.

The sun plays chase and catch amongst the clouds
as gusts run shadows upwards, through the cliffs.
Our boat at anchor tugs to get ashore
to join the pack of hikers in the vale.

## The Hamam

In sandals, a cotton towel around my waist,
I'm led to a large room surrounded by a marble bench
and eight marble basins, each with hot
and cold-water faucets.
The centre of the room is taken up
by a large marble platform.

The masseur, clad as I,
leads me to sit by a large basin of water.
He gently pours panfuls of warm water
over my head and shoulders, then hands me the metal pan
to continue, while he pours hot water from another basin
over the platform to warm the marble.
He then leads me to the platform
and removes my towel and sandals.
He places the towel on the platform
and directs me to lie face down on the towel.

Starting with my feet and toes, the young man scrubs my
entire body with a rough glove.
The experience is surprisingly pleasant.
Then he rinses and lathers, covering me in thick rich suds.
He rinses again. I roll over.
He repeats the process toe to head.

I stand for a gentle rubdown with dry towels before being led
to the cooling room, where I lie on a couch covered in towels.

After ten minutes, the masseur takes me to a smaller room
with a massage table. There he massages my entire body
with rose oil for forty minutes – toes, fingers, ear lobes,
temples, every muscle back to front.

I spend the remainder of the day
luxuriating on a couch by the Dalaman River.

## Fethiye Morning

Hibiscus orchestrates oranges and lemons,
hanging in profusion above cobbled streets.
Roses, pink and red, strut amongst the bougainvillea.
From a cypress, high above the date palms,
dove coos his love call in the morning sun.

Mothers, scarved and shawled,
lead tykes in sky-blue smocks.
Girls with pink backpacks chatter gaily,
flocking slowly to school.

Older boys and young men stroll arm in arm.
Men in business suits greet and congregate
with kisses on both cheeks.


## Fethiye Bay

Tables by a waterfall,
soft breezes from the bay,
hot bowls of lentil soup with crusty rolls:
While we dip our bread, sip Turkish beer,
and watch the men at play,
the scent of sweet tobacco fills the air.

Beads flow through work-worn fingers;
dice clatter on the boards;
backgammon pieces move from side to side:
It's lunch hour in the marketplace
on a warm day in the sun.
Our gulet lies at anchor on the tide.

*gulet – Turkish motorsailer of mahogany and teak,
16-35 m in length.*

## Night Before Sailing

Ah, what a gift to lie beneath
so many spires of masts,
spread vertically, crossed in dazzling white
beneath the stars!

Ah, what a gift to see the moon
reflected on the bay,
to feel the gentle sway against the swell,
to know all's well
the night before we sail on azure seas.

Tonight we sleep
beneath the scuttles' friendly glow,
all snuggled in our cabin bunks below.

## Early Morning in Port

The pale blue sky is puffed with early mist;
good morning rooster pipes the start of day:
The first to rise, I sprawl upon the deck,
excited that we'll soon be on our way.

Two seagulls stand loud watch upon the prow.
The hour's yet too early by the clock.
An eager sailor ploughs across our bow;
while commerce purrs to life beyond the dock.

At last, the crew's about and on the deck.
The patroon makes his rounds; the day's begun.
Soon breakfast is on the stove and all is well.
and we'll be out before the noon day sun.

*\* patroon – ship's captain - owner*

## Contemplating the Rocky Coast

Oh, if these stones had tongues to speak,
what stories they would tell!
Of grizzly saints and warrior kings
and hermits' huts amongst the crags.

'Midst these same rocks lived men of iron
who hunted with the spear.
And pilgrims came from countries far
to worship without fear.

From these rough shores the world was found
by men who dared the waves
and faced the Barbary pirates,
who dragged many off as slaves.

'And oh, these stones would tell much more,
if only they had tongues to speak.

## Kekova Bay

Heaven's candles sparkle on the mirror of the bay;
The haloed moon reflects her milky tones.
My face is all-a-tingle from the sun and salted spray.
Our sleeping vessel shifts her creaking bones.

Love and laughter echo 'round the table on the bow.
Evening breezes whisper 'mongst the sails.
Small waves slap, tickle at the hull beneath the prow
as I stand to taste the magic at the rail.

## Kale and Simena

'Neath the crystal waters
stand the ruins of a town.
where ancient people bought and sold their wares.
What tragedy of nature
sent great temples tumbling down
and brought the ocean flooding through their homes?

What men then built their castles
on high cliffs above the bay,
who lifted rocks impossible to haul?
Were they killed in battle
on some single valiant day?
Or did they fall in illness or decay?

Great wealth erects tall cities.
Proud men build great tombs.
Monuments stand shining in the sun.
Yet Nature is the ruler
and Time sets all the rules.
Men are soon forgotten when they're done.


## Merchants of Kas

Senol from Mount Ararat sells carpets from home.
He travels the world with his wares,
while Halil Tufan tailors shirts in his shop,
where he makes alterations with care.
He sells cloths of all colours to fit every taste,
Mediterranean blue and white stripe.

Other shops display spices and Turkish delights,
blue hand-painted tiles and warm wraps for the night,
silver bracelets and pendants with fine jewels to charm,
ceramic blue eyes meant to ward off all harm.
It's hard to resist such fabulous sights.
No tourist can leave here in haste.

## Café in Kas

My love and I fold into cushioned plastic
'neath Efes Pilsen umbrellas
and the generous shade of a large mulberry.

High on an overhanging balcony,
beyond the zakkum pink blossoms,
a ginger cat luxuriates.

The narrow cobble alley buzzes
a harmonious babble of German, English, Turkish.
Efes beer slides down smoothly.

On the square, Ataturk stands watch.
In the harbour, boats of gleaming wood are docked;
their fittings sparkle stainless steel.

A sleeping dog does not give way
to scooters zigging about in impossible places.

No skateboards here:
It will remain so – insha'Allah!

*insha'Allah – God willing*

## Kas to Antalya by Dolmus

Below the necklace mountain road,
green robe flows smocked with strips of gold.
Silver tassels line her winding hem.
Here goats and shepherds stroll amongst rocks,
where tombs and broken sarcophagi lie.
Here and there, like sapphire pins,
minarets sprout 'midst row upon row of fruit and nut,
all speck'd with poppies.

We glide down to Demre on the bay
where greenhouse roofs spread their ugly stains.
As far as the eye can see: tomatoes for the world.
Then, back on mountain paths,
we crawl 'round hairpin curves
on cliffs of gold above the sea.


## The Carpet Seller

Sweet tea and thick coffee
waver our resolve.
Rug, over rug, over rug,
displays hours, months, years
of nimble finger dedication.
Now they're a gift of love
at "dead horse" prices.

Though much money has filled my palms,
I shall die poor in the wealth of this world.
I am rich only in friends
and in the joy of such fine art.

Art is love.
Love has no price.

## The Carpet Weaver

Ah, what art my nimble fingers weave,
in bright arrays of wool in countless hues,
in finest silks, during months of toil.
Since I was four, my mother taught me all.

My tapestries of fireworks live and breathe
with secret codes and messages of joy.
Knots – a million-fold – all tell their tales
of love, of hope, of many broken hearts.

These are the treasures I give to you:
the jewels of a woman's love for home and kin.

## Aspendos Theatre

In Aspendos, the Romans built a theatre for their sport
where gladiators died to please the crowd.
Here frantic lions and leopards
tore their victims limb from limb,
and blood spectators screamed their pleasure loud.

And now, Vivaldi, Haydn, Bach, Mozart fill the stands,
symphonic strains beneath the evening sky.
When gentle youth play strings and brass upon a carpet red,
the Turkish moon brings moisture to my eye.

## Perge, Astendos, and Side

Two thousand years ago...

a hundred thousand slaves built baths
with walls of gleaming tile
where Roman rulers soaked away their cares
and had their bodies rubbed with oil
while indulging in fine wines
and planning further conquests with their peers.

Two thousand years ago...

the miles of aqueduct built high
on columned arches great
brought water from the mountain top
down to the city gate
where marble fountains pleased the eye
and cooled the city streets
while irrigating home and shop
and making latrines sweet.

Two thousand years ago...

the women went to market,
gossiped on the square
while servants nursed the babies
and combed the children's hair.
With slaves for almost every task,
 the soldier's wives were free
to weave and sew and spin fine wools
as pleasing as could be.
Fine horses, sheep, and household pets
were valued with great pride
but slaves were cheaply bought and sold
and toiled 'til they died.

        Two thousand years ago... chances are...
        I would have been a slave!

## Kapadokya

There's a vale of fairy chimneys
decked with magic windows small,
Some look like men with great stone hats,
and some like mushrooms tall.

Here the Hattis, then the Hittites
built homes in hills of stone.
Concealed from their enemies,
they made these caves their home.

The Phrygians and the Persians
came later to these lands.
They burrowed deep into the rock
with chisels and bare hands.

When Christians fled Jerusalem
from Roman sword and spear,
they built their churches underground
to worship free from fear.

Byzantine monks made frescoes
with paints for all to view,
to illustrate to pilgrims
the tenets they held true.

When Islam flared from desert sands
the Seljuks brought the flame.
The Ottomans held high their swords
to spread the Muslim name.

Once beautiful white horses
ran free upon this plain.
And snow-white doves brought news of love
and peace to end all pain.

## Türkiye

This Turkey is a magic land,
a womb of humankind
where poets and philosophers
informed the searching mind.

Assyrians gave us writing,
Byzantines left us their art,
while artisans of every sort
contributed their part.

The Hittites were great potters.
Persian rugs remain the best.
The Seljuks fashioned gold and jewels.
Mother Nature did the rest.

Turkish farmers, just as long ago,
still take the country roads.
Their women still wear scarves of white;
and donkeys bear great loads.

They carry figs, plums, olives,
dates, and oranges in sacks.
The men walk on, their staffs in hand,
their goods upon their backs.

Beside the roads, the cypress trees
all coo with turtle doves.
Throughout the land, they echo loud
their songs of lasting love.

These doves are still the symbols,
their olive twigs held high,
of wondrous peace for all the world,
as long as they shall fly.

## Hoscakal

On our last night in Turkey, we dined 'neath the moon
while a dervish whirled into a trance
to the strings of an ud and their soft lilting tune,
with the beat of a def to enhance.

It's farewell to old Turkey, her fabulous places,
her carpets, her teas, and such welcoming graces,
her friendship, her love, and those beautiful faces,
her music, her food, her romance.

Gelecek sefer görüiürüz.  (Until next time)

# Greece

## Portrait Unpainted  –  Naoussa, Paros

Were I to paint the scene from here,
beneath the tamarisk trees,
I'd pick a bright palette
and let the colours run.

For upper sky, cerulean,
violet for the bay:
with touches of cobalt,
turquoise and ultramarine.

Then for the rocks and sand,
I'd choose a wash of sparkling grey,
light ochre, burnt sienna
patched with olive, sap green, and sun
to keep the picture warm.

In the light and pleasant breeze,
I'd trim the whitewashed houses
all in bird's egg blue,
with rows and rows of olive trees.

Yet, could I paint the joyful sounds
of singing birds, music,
laughter and children on the beach,
and tinkling waves upon the shore?

How could I paint
the perfumed mix
of salt and fish
and sunscreen on my nose?

I can't.

You must come for yourself
and spend a week or more.

## Sands and Rocks
## (overlooking the Aegean Sea)

We stroll along a dusty road
'neath robin egg sky,
by flowered bushes
and murmuring sea.
Tiny birds flutter on rock-brown hills.
Crates of grapes, stacked high,
promise sweet muscatel.

In ten minutes, the scene changes.
We stroll on yellow sand
and snap pictures:
blue-domed chapels,
houses like white cubes
among the scatterings of rock.
Farther out,
frothy lines slosh along the rocky shore.

Then, a potpourri:
pink blossoms, sheltering palms,
and brown goats grazing tufts
of sundry hay on stony hills
near our parasol.

## Swimming in the Aegean Sea

Necks all fluffed out in cool breeze,
seagulls bob on tiny waves.
Sea murmurs her seductive invitation.
I accept. I rise and fall with the waves
and float content.

Snuggled like a seagull
on her ample bosom,
I feel the sea's warm breath.
The myriad floods of turmoil
From across the sea concern me not.

## A Culinary Curiosity

Here in the Greek islands,
octopus and squid hang in rows
by wharf-side restaurants.
Bare-chested fishermen have beaten them,
but only to the point of tenderness.

In local shops and restaurants,
bottles of dry wine are sold.
Dancing feet have pressed the grapes
but left the seeds uncrushed - almost.

Without the fishermen's skill,
the octopus and squid would be too tough.
Without the seeds' bitter tannin,
wine would be too sweet.

A culinary curiosity:
For tenderness and flavour,
violence is often necessary.
Yet only just enough.

## Winds Across the Bay

Warm Nor'-wester
roars across Naoussa Bay,
herding fluffy white clouds,
tugging at papers and hats,
and tipping over half-filled glasses.

In the shelter of the harbour,
fishing boats tug and dance
at their moorings.

Look up,
in all the vast blue sky,
not a seagull to be seen.
Swimmers

With languid strokes,
a pair of blue-haired ladies glide.
One, wearing a top of purple flowers,
does the crawl.
The other, floating on her back,
kicks her feet, and fins.
Like pallid water wings,
her bare breasts float on either side.

Waist-deep in the blue-green sea,
a balding bundle of skin and bones
does calisthenics.
He flaps his water wings as though to fly,
then sits up to his neck in brine
and sighs contentedly.

Clattering as they go,
three old crones wearing hats,
swim way, way out
until I can hardly see them.

A flock
of shouting, unclothed children
fly along the beach.

Like a seal,
a boy swims underwater in the sparkling bay;
more bronze-skinned urchins,
almost dolphins,
with endless energy and enthusiasm,
dive from a rock.

Ah, youth!

## All Is One

Saint Helena found the Saviour's cross on Calvary.
Then, between Constantinople and Rome,
stopped at Paros, Greece, to escape a storm.

Now, every year, the faithful honour her.
In her name, they carry sprigs of basil.
Ah! The fragrance.

History, culture, religion:
All is intertwined.

## Naoussa Rocks: A Weather Report

Near storm's end:
An orange cat sits grumpily,
soaking in the rain.
Grey clouds lower their veils
and scatter on the wind.
Silver streaks dance across the bay.
The sea sighs.

After the storm:
Tree branches shed their tears.
Marble terraces gleam happily in the sunshine.
Soon ...having quenched their thirst,
green shoots will spring refreshed
from sun-baked fields.

Everywhere, the air fills with perfume --
cypress, cinnamon, carnation, coffee,
peppercorn, basil, church incense,
oleander with the sweet smell of vanilla.
Funny how smells are so intense
after a storm.

Tonight, on the cathedral square,
people will sing and dance.
Life goes on.

## It's All Greek to Me

My body language won't speak Greek.

"Yes" is "nah";
yet my head shakes "no."

"No" is "okhee":
but I nod affirmative.

I can't control the reflexes
of life-learned speech.

As the years fly by,
change becomes more difficult.


## A Simple Rainstorm

Lightning flashes in the distance;
a mighty breath blows up from the sea,
scattering pages from my hypergraphic scribbles.
While I give chase,
dark clouds rumble
and open in an instant.

The wind whips up white-maned waves,
like magnificent, bucking stallions.
Necklaces of water tumble from the heavens;
stridently, they fall upon the table outside our door.
Then, as suddenly as it arrives,
the storm departs.

Bathed in tears, all in a row,
trees in silver-leafed olive orchards
smile and glisten.

Once more, the sea turns scintillating blue.
Stones, once dusty brown, glimmer rose-red.
Pine resin fills the air with balm.

## Yin and Yang

Amongst blue, yellow, and red limestone houses,
Athenian dukes laid narrow cobblestone streets.
On high hills, they used columns from quake-felled shrines to
build castles, forts, and churches.

Then, the Muslims seized the land,
And everything was simplified.
Peasants crushed limestone blocks
to sanitize white-walled homes.

The complexity of Christianity
yielded to the simplicity of Islam.
The two halves of one:
yin met yang.

## Peace Comes Dropping Slow

At 2:00AM,
what could be more noisy
than an Athens hotel room? --
shouts, blaring horns, rattling air conditioners,
rumbling motorcycles, and droning buses.

At 8:00AM,
laundry flutters on lines in the wind
'midst antennae and potted greenery.
While shirtless men sip coffee on cluttered balconies,
countless voices join the babble from the street below.

At 4:00PM,
Frank Sinatra croons in the lobby
over the chatter of cell phones
and the click-clack of tiny wheels on tile.

It's all so out-of-place:
Here, in the cradle of philosophy,
peace comes dropping slowly.

## Impossible Achievements (Athens)

What a tiny creature is man.
How powerful his will.
Throughout the ages,
he builds his massive monuments.

His motives:
to demonstrate his power,
to be remembered,
to worship his gods.

Man's achievements are
so impossible.
And so achievable.


## The Con Artist

A French "tourist" approaches,
map in hand,
"Monsieur, vous parlez français?"

Why me, an obvious tourist?

Of course, I answer, "Oui."

Accomplices cruise in from side and rear.
My companion ordered me away.
Panicked, I obey.

When people use your kindness against you,
the world is evil indeed.

# Italy

## Piazza San Marco, Venice

From the massive railway station,
just across the causeway bridge
labelled Ponté Della Liberta,
we cross canals on slender pontés,
stroll for hours through narrow alleys
past the many hundred shops
and small cafés with sidewalk tables,
little squares with ancient churches,
then across the Grande Canale,
following signs "Piazza San Marco"
as anticipation rises.

Soon we hear the church bells chiming,
spy the lofty Campanile *
in view of the Clock Tower.
towering high above the Piazza.
Step into the great basilica,
through the arches dimmed in shadow,
gaze in awe at ancient splendour
tiled with multi-coloured stones on the floors.
On walls and ceilings
saints and sinners tiled in gold.

And my heart stands still a moment
as the bronze Moors strike the hour.

*** bell tower**

## Puccini

In Venice, at the Church of San Giovanni,
my love and I heard arias by Puccini
voiced by Fabiola Formiga, soprano,
and the blind tenor, Riccardo Buoncristiani.
If we could, we'd be back there molto presto
per sentire più cosa migliore
e canzoni favorite Neapolitano.

## The Parade of Life

We sit and watch the great parade:
f tourists led in docile groups,
cameras clicking as they go.
Lines of children, two-by-two,
led by nuns in flowing robes.
Hurry, hurry, much to see!
No time to stop and taste the air.

Families on holidays,
with children still too young for school,
but not too young for sights and sounds.
Fresh lovers on their honeymoons,
And couples in their golden years:
with time to give and time to share.

A few, with slower schedules,
stand and gaze in awe
at sculptures on the archway posts
beside the square.
Students on sabbatical,
their livings in their knapsacks,
roam, wandering
curious, pad in hand.

Contented on our sidewalk bench,
we watch the happy world pass by.
We hear the joyful sounds of life
and feel contentment for our lot.

## The Sacred and the Profane

In a borrowed church
adjacent to St. Mark's Cathedral square,
bearded priest with palms together,
reverently leads his tiny flock.
Orthodox, in minor fifths,
they genuflect and chant their prayers.

Then, as incense floats about,
sanctifying Holy Books,
blessing relics and sacred ikons,
white-veiled women cross themselves
and utter treble-voiced responses
to the chanted sacred prayers.

The rustling of the women's dresses
sounds like small birds on the wing.
The women kneel and then they rise,
     kneel and rise,
     kneel and rise
as prayers ascend on clouds of incense
to their God above the skies.

## Venice Gliding

Serenaded from above,
in soft, multi-voiced Italian,
accompanied by violins and accordions,
my love and I glide in a gondola,
royalty on velvet cushions
in the Venetian moonlight.

All along the narrow causeways,
'neath sculptured bridges,
sea water laps low at the steps.
Everywhere, joyful tourists sip wine.
We are in love;
we can't help it.

## The Cathedral

Not as tourists,
but as simple pilgrims,
we enter the jewel that is St. Mark's.
Blazing with light
and dressed in shining gold,
the ceilings gleam brilliant mosaics.

A priest leads the chants and psalms.
An irony: the medieval Latin is new to many;
yet everyone sings.
And the Italian tongue,
gently, softly, it flows with love,
the melodies familiar to all.

In the massive square before the cathedral,
church bells ring
while pigeons flutter over the crowds.
To prove they came here,
tourists photograph each other;
while their children scale the backs of ancient lions.

On grand piano, strings, and accordion,
musicians play world music in the square.
Ten euros for a demitasse of coffee,
To sit for such a sum or stand for free.
On a sunny afternoon like this,
a coffee could last an hour or more.

In Venice on a Sunday afternoon,
music is everywhere.

Here, two worlds dwell side by side
in complete harmony:
the sacred and the profane,
as all great art should be.

## Sunday in Florence

Crowds are everywhere in Florence.
On single-file sidewalks,
people walk four-abreast.
On narrow, cobblestone streets,
built for horses and pedestrians
over nine hundred years ago,
autos and motor scooters jounce about.

Impoverished Gypsy women
lie ragged and prostrate
on sidewalks and in church doorways.
The rest of us, much better dressed,
all look the same
and get along.
Italian, English, German, French
languages no longer matter.

On church walls, in civic buildings, in museums,
ancient statues and paintings appear everywhere.
Inside the churches and great halls,
the walls and ceilings gleam
with frescoes, panels, and murals.
The amazing Fifteenth Century detail
leaves the viewer awestruck.

In the piazzas,
hawkers display mass-produced paintings,
sold to gullible tourists at can't resist prices.
Others sketch caricatures
for those who like to see their own image
as remembrance of places visited.
In the great cathedral,
we gather close in wooden stalls.
'Round the altar,
'neath the painted dome and stained glass,
tall candles flicker.
While the organ plays Pallestrina,

the church bells announce High Mass.
In tones so soft,
a gentle, white-haired priest
invites the people to worship.
We don't need to know his tongue
to feel his love.
The Mass begins.

An a cappella choir intones *Asperges Mei*.
Throughout this cathedral's vast expanse,
the old, familiar Latin echoes and re-echoes.
from a hundred hidden nooks as if the statues sing.

## Past and Present: A Meditation

On a day of blue skies, shade trees,
and lovers, pigeons strut the hot pavement,
waiting for crumbs.
Beside the road,
two yellow butterflies play tag over the dewy grass.

Leisurely, we stroll the four-kilometre battlement,
surrounding Lucca.
At a bench with a view,
we pause for cheese and grapes
and happy conversation.

Last night, as before, I supped on pasta,
assaulted, boiled in salt --
too much for my tender tongue.
Thank God for hearty breakfasts!
Tonight, in cheerful company,
I shall dine on steak and wine.

I move through the past;
I move through the present.
Despite its culinary inconveniences,
the present seems better to me.
'Way back at the battlements,
I wonder how the soldiers dined.

## Smoke and Rain

During a sudden Italian downpour,
we stop at a tabaccheria
and lock up our bicycles.
The company is loud and jovial;
everyone sips grappa, caffè gran crema, and Moretti.

Though smokers stand at the door,
the rain drives their smoke inside.
Yet no one minds;
everyone's happy.

The water table had been critically low.

## Cathedral San Martino

Camera-happy tourists follow loud-voiced guides
to view parts of great cathedrals in dim light.
We return on Sunday morning, not as tourists,
to be treated to full view, an awesome sight:
stained-glass windows bathed in sunshine,
countless frescoes, statues tall,
full-voiced organ and a polyphonic choir,
voicing melodies familiar in a language full of life,
and once more my heart is bursting at the sound.

Amiomo questo luogo - dovremo tomore.
*(We love it here; we'll have to come again.)*

## So Little Time

Florence:
How can I possibly describe this city of
Michelangelo, Boticelli, Fra Lippolippi
Fra Angelica, Caravaggio, Dürer, Dante
and famous pizza?

So much to see and do.
So little time.

A Florentian meditation:
At the end of their lives,
how many have that gnawing feeling
that they haven't experienced
all they intended to experience.

Yet ...
Is such fulfillment even possible?

## Some Rain and Good Food

Yesterday we cycled in the rain;
a sudden downpour soaked us for a while.
We each bought an umbrella
then the sun came out.
Within an hour, our clothes were dry again.

We found a pizzaria with good food;
my faith in seafood pasta was restored.
"Spaghetti scholios, mi piace molto." *(I like very much)*
I ask for "po' sele" *(little salt)*
and it's good.

## Florence: Beauty and Bathrooms

Pizzas made to order by the chef:
Bruschetta, Panini.
Spaghetti with thick tomato sauce;
spaghetti with seafood:
best ever.

Local wines and Birra Moretti:
king size.
Bus rides through the Tuscan hills,
above the city.
A stop at a Franciscan monastery:
monks chant the Divine Office
in Latin.

The top of the Duomo:
four hundred and sixty-three steps.
Gold, silver, and jewellery shops,
on the Ponte Vacchio:
the only bridge not bombed by the Germans
in World War II.

The cathedral organ after Sunday Mass:
J. S. Bach's *Toccata and Fugue in D Minor*.
Everywhere we go:
friendly and helpful people,
parents and children alike.

Yet ...
nothing is perfect.
We return to our hotel room,
with its tiny bathroom
and strange little shower
right in the middle.

Tell me:
What would life be without its dualities?

## Le Cinque Terra

Railway
hugs the jagged coast from Riomaggiore,
teasing between tunnels
with glimpses of sparkling sea.

We descend at Monterosso,
beneath cliffside houses and hotels,
to a strip of pebbly beach.
Oily bodies sprawl,
drink beer,
listen to loud music
and puff cigarettes.

We're not impressed
and flee by boat to Vernazza,
where houses perch
like eagles on the granite crags
above the boiling sea.
Backpack hikers descend
the heaving gangplank ahead of us
to climb steep narrow streets
between the shops and cafés
and find a stony pathway to the sky.

Another wave-rocked boat-ride
sets us down at Manarola
where bathers cover every inch of rocks
around the harbour
like seals barking in the sun and spray.

We pay an entrance fee
to walk the graffiti filled
"Tunnel of Love"
to a cliffside path,
Riomaggione,
and the train.

## Arrivederci Roma

I have visited the geographical crossroads of the world;
stood in wonder beneath the bleak dome
of the Hagia Sophia in Constantinople (Istanbul);
knelt in reverent awe in Saint Peter's Basilica in Rome.

I have climbed the ruins of the once mighty
Pantheon in Athens;
circled the Colliseum and vast ruins
of once Imperial Rome; sat breathless beneath
Michaelangelo's glorious frescoes
in the Sistine Chapel.

I have witnessed
the genius of great sculptors, painters,
builders and musicians. My heart beat faster.
I was filled with indescribable elation.

One might eventually forget
the individual experiences
of beauty and history,
but... all those joys
enter the bloodstream.

Their influence
is bound to remain
forever.


## Sorrento

Cafes and narrow laneways
alive with music;
accordion, guitar, mandolin –
O Solo Mio, Tarantella.
Gentle, happy voices in the moonlight.
Sorrento in love.

## Sorrento Evening

Hazy moon peeps over harbour,
twinkling lights, light breeze.
Air warm, verge of October.

Beneath Versuvius' shadow
cruise ship at anchor,
tenders putter
tourist lines;

tour-guides,
signs held high,
"Seguami", "Follow me", "Suivez-moi",
busy streets, alleyways.

Sidewalk cafes,
wine and pasta, pizza, calamari.
Happy children stroll – mini-lovers, hand-held,
*madre, padre, nonno, nonna.*

Sun-kissed from the beach,
we recall buoyancy
kept us finning crystal waters
*Bay of San Francesco.*

*Volaviamare* from Capri;
our turn on the list.
The world goes on
without us.

## Sorrento Haiku

Every step down hill
will require two in return.
Price paid to explore.

Narrow little lane,
"beep, beep" around the corner;
room for only one.

On the ballistrades,
we sit to enjoy the view
above the harbour.

In the brilliant light,
three dozen buoys in the bay
mark the shrimp trap lines.

Before the vista
tourists pose for photographs,
blocking out the view.

First he'll comb his hair,
try a different pose or two,
proving he was here.

Sparkling 'cross the bay,
Versuvius in the morning
frames the tourist's smile.

"See this photograph,
Versuvius behind me
on our latest trip."

All along the rail
tourist backsides hide our view.
Soon they'll move along.

Hydrofoil returns
with her load of passengers,
sun-basked tourists all.

Brisk accordion,
every note a memory,
well-known aria.

O Solo Mio
sung as if a heart will break,
Caro mio ben.

Sad the church bell tolls,
bringing us to prayerful thought,
thankful for the day.

## Menu

Cocktail di amber,
prfosciutto e melone,
succo di frutta.

Panino misto
formaggio e cipolle,
vino locale.


## The People of Capri

warm, unpretentious, friendly,
patient drivers, few car horns blaring.
Bus drivers
miracles workers with sharp corners;
two buses pass through the eye of a needle
in opposition
in tune

Bed & Breakfasts
mere steps from Marina Grande
and excellent beach.
the steps:
one hundred and twenty-three,
up hill,
both ways.

## Victorrio

Imagine living on the side of a mountain.
Every morning you take 120 stairs
down to the harbour to see how the world is doing.

You buy bread, cheese, tomatoes, grapes and beer.
Perhaps you also buy a bottle of wine.
Then you climb the same steps,
one small shopping bag in each hand. Up, up, up.
You pause part way to see the vista.

Laundry flutters from balconies
above a narrow alleyway.
The blue Mediterranean glitters beyond.

Victorrio climbs these same steps
two or three times every day.
At 78, he's fit and jovial.

Maybe we should stay here longer


## Cure for Vertigo

On the Isle of Capri,
take the chair lift to the top of Monte Salaro.
At 589 meters,
you will be rewarded
with a panoramic view
of the Bay of Naples,
the Bay of Salerno
and the entire Island of Capri.

Some sturdier souls walk back from the summit
via the 14th Century Carthusian hermitage.

We returned as we had come,
by chair lift – a definite cure for vertigo.

## Naples

Naples, city of sad love stories.
Today, she's a grand old lady
whose make-up is streaked, undone.
Streets garbage-strewn;
Infrastructure, buildings in need of repair.
Once-glorious gardens appear
forsaken,
weed-infested.

Despite hardship and poverty,
children play, kick soccer balls
from wall to wall in church squares.
Families stroll, greeting acquaintances.
An accordion plays at a sidewalk café.

High on the hill, above the city,
Quartiere Vomero stands as a city within a city.
Here, inhabitants have risen in opulence
above grime and struggle of lower town.
Yet, even here, amidst the beauty,
a burned-out car-wreck sits abandoned
on the main thoroughfare.

# South America

# Rio de Janeiro

## A Samba Party

In the favela,
I'm suddenly surrounded,
twelve to fifteen deep.
Barefoot urchins plead
with eyes as big as birds' eggs –
a language no tongue may deny.
Small hands grope and grab
at arms, legs, pockets.
I break free.
To grant the smallest alms would court disaster.

A hundred drums and shouting voices,
amplified over giant speakers,
proclaim the Samba Celebration.
Thousands gyrate around the great favela hall.

With arms outstretched over the city,
Christ the Redeemer looks down
upon all his people.


## Copa Cabana Beach

In the sweltering November summer,
Far beyond the smoky horizon,
waves crash
and send up messages
of golden foam
on a hazy stretch of burning sand.

Copa Cabana Beach is like that.

# Buenos Aires

## Buenos Aires in November

Massive, wide avenues
link to narrow, cobbled streets.
Mauve jacarda blossoms blow in the breeze.
We sit at a table in the square,
pour beer from two-litre bottles
and crack peanuts in the shell.

Men greet men with kisses on the cheek.
Lovers embrace unashamedly
on a park bench.
Free-range school kids run about
in white lab coats.
Art, antiques, and tango
are everywhere under the sun.

Great wealth and poverty,
beauty and decay.
Buenos Aires is a city of dualities.
She is ours to explore:

her people, her charm,
her music, her stories,
her soul.

## Ode to the Cementerio Recoleta

Feral cats patrol avenues and narrow lanes
of crumbling mausoleums.
Magnificent gloss-black tombs
hold faded caskets
with rusted handles,
cracked plaster,
shattered stained glass.
Wealthy corpses molder in dust
of wilted flowers
and broken vases.
Rats and birds crap just as freely
on rich and poor.

When I die, build me a hostel
for orphans,
urchins,
homeless waifs.
Write not my eulogy in stone
but on the hearts and lips
of children not yet born.
Cast my ashes to the wind;
I'd not be happy here.

## Plaza Dorrego

A Media Luz (By Half Light):
Tango dancers flutter,
butterflies in the afternoon sun.
Plaza Dorrego comes to life at four.

Miguel hammers centavo coins,
little concave disks to dangle
from earlobe or wrist,
to jangle on a gaucho's belt.

A toddler teases pigeons in giddy circles.
Grandmother sits, legs akimbo, fanning her brow.
Motorcycles putter, car horns bleep.
Policeman on the corner stands asleep.

Ode to the Cementerio Recoleta

Feral cats patrol avenues and narrow lanes
of crumbling mausoleums.
Magnificent gloss-black tombs
hold faded caskets
with rusted handles,
cracked plaster,
shattered stained glass.
Wealthy corpses moulder in dust
of wilted flowers
and broken vases.
Rats and birds crap just as freely
on rich and poor.

When I die, build me a hostel
for orphans, urchins, homeless waifs.
Write not my eulogy in stone
but on the hearts and lips
of children not yet born.
Cast my ashes to the wind;
I'd not be happy here.

## Manuela

Yesterday, Manuella,
at a café on Florida Street by Centro Pacifica,
I sat at a sidewalk table,
in the company of prosperous Porteños
and pampered tourists.
I sipped Quilmes
and ate zucchini, fried greens,
and filet mignon wrapped in bacon strips.

You sat on the sidewalk too,
around the corner, at the curb,
an angel with shabby wings,
seven-year-old mother to a baby brother,
both unbathed, unschooled,
unhoused, unfed.

bed of dirt and rags, beneath a leaky roof.

What will become of you Manuella
as the tourists pass you by.
Who will love your baby brother?

How dare I ask when I eat so well in your city,
around the corner from where you sit,
silently pleading?

You are myriad, Manuella,
on the streets of Buenos Aires,
in the subte,
in the villas miserias.

Last night you visited me in a dream.
I tried to help you.
My stomach had turned to stone.

# Mexico

# Mayan Peninsula

## White Sands

Hundreds of millions of years ago,
unique and unremarked,
a myriad of tiny mollusks lived out their lives,
then died.

Over time,
their sun-bleached shells,
surf-clawed into bits of bone,
are slammed to shore
with the crashing tide.

I too am a speck of life,
a mere flicker on the beach.
On the razor's edge of *Now*,
I lie on the sparkling sand.

## My Heart Is Full

Hulls of orange, purple,
banana yellow, lime green.
Striped sails billowing and pulling,
the sailboats glide,
like quetzel feathers on aquamarine.
Frothy white sparkles splash my feet.

My love emerges from the water,
dripping, sun-kissed,
with her shell earrings,
necklace of snowy pearl,
and emerald swim dress.
Silver hair glistening in the morning sun,
warmer than all the sand and sea,
she smiles.

## Tiptoe Eyes

Waves wash over the coral reef.
A naked toddler digs in the sand;
her mother basks, topless.

Daddy builds a castle with a moat.
Young son scoops out a hole;
soon he'll drain the ocean.

Ensconced beneath her parasol,
with Chatelaine and gold-tipped cigarette,
maman sits not far away,

In the ocean's gentle ripple,
three Mayan cleaners rake the seaweed,
dawn to dusk.

Lie back to dream.
Tiptoe through sandy foam.
Drift with the waves.

In ten million miles of solitude,
five gulls float below wisps of cloud,
and myriad silver urchins
swarm in gardens
beneath the sea.

Under my thatch,
as the ocean strokes my tired ears,
I laze through sun-filled hours.

At last,
my city pressures –
computer, fax, phone, and wild, wild commute –
evaporate in the sun.

## Of Daydreams and Seaweed

From bitter memories of snow and ice,
Sleet, fog and rain, and traffic screams,
I waken to a beach of golden sand
and breathe deep of the sea's perfume –
honeyed air of the Mayan coast.

Peek-a-boo morning sun rises swiftly
to cross the Caribbean sky.
Now and then it hides
behind fluffy grey-white puffs of cloud –
only to blaze forth, promising the day's heat.

As far as I can daydream,
I see soothing blue.
Grandma in her sunhat looks for shells.
Fair-skinned toddlers race in the surf.
Bikini maidens chat along the shore.

Stiff breeze sets hats flying
across the mottled sand.
Cormorant swoops and dives
for breakfast on the waves.
Jogger puffs off last night's revelry,
ogles topless beauties on the beach,
reminiscing, perhaps, of loves gone by.

Then,
I see them:
As sports fishers
troll beyond the reef
and kayaks glide in tandem
past snorkeling youth,
the beach's only Mayans
rake seaweed into orange barrows.

## Oaxaca City

### Oaxaca Weaver

see her now
by pink adobe wall
beneath bougainvillea orange

knees sway on mat of faded reed
between column and loom
back straps taut
her small dark fingers flit
back - forth, back - forth
her shuttle glides

carded wool - purple, green
indigo tint of heaven
pale gold of sacred hummingbird
eagle wing
breeze of eternity
scattering of stars
teardrops of the moon
robozo for a new mother

### Chiclets

wide-eyed waif with pleading smile
Chiclets on a tray
"un peso, un peso."
with silent persistence
her six or seven years sear my gilded world
of molè con pollo and dark beer

her little friend at table lip
just as sweet
innocent trust in pairs
two smiles warmer than all Oaxaca sunshine

"peso, si.  peso, si."
and slice of salted lime
momentary happiness

## The Zocalo

on the great expanse
before the cathedral terrace
i hear church bells chime

in the Zocalo
reed pipes and whistles
guitars and trumpets
drums and cymbals
and mariachi voices
sound their ancient rhythms

wares jiggle multi-textured
on men's shoulders
on women's heads
baskets sway

roses and gardenias
spices and buns
perfume the air, everywhere,
bangles and beads
rugs and rebozos
dazzle the eyes

a dozen tongues or more
enter my wrinkled mind
and children laugh and run
bouncing balloons high
to touch the moon
sweethearts cuddle and kiss
with star-bright eyes
unashamed
for in the zocalo
love is in fashion

on the great expanse
before the cathedral terrace
i hear church bells chime
and all of this.....is love

## Quétzalcoatl

at Cholula, beyond the smoking mountains,
you sat in sacred effigy,
with your yellow face,
red beak,
feather mantle, red, white, black,
butterfly jewel,
diadem crown.
and on your feet,
gold socks,
golden sandals.
Quet-zal-coatl.

to you, mighty wind god,
we gave our fairest youth.
in forty days of feast and birdlike dance,
he honoured you
and then, upon your holy altar,
we gave you his heart.

his flesh became your flesh.
in sacred union,
we ate your body
and drank your blood.

you died by proxy
and rose again.
in your rising,
we were born again.
but you despised our offering.
as you yourself had prophesied,
you returned,
as bearded warriors in gleaming helmets,
seeking gold.
then, in your fury, you made war
with mighty Tez-cat-lipoca,
Smoking Mirror,
king of gods,
and with Vit-zil-op-ochli,

the Hummingbird, the mighty war god.
daily, we offered many hearts
of youths and slaves and captive warriors
to hurry Smoking Mirror
in your defeat.
with fiery thunder-sticks
you smashed our altars,
threw down our gods,
laid waste our cities of stone,
and burned our sacred books.

you planted foreign gods
in dome-topped temples.

while waging lesser wars,
Smoking Mirror swore revenge.
four hundred years flew by.
humming bird rested.

emerging from the dust of pathways north,
the conquering helmets took new form
with foreign names:
Pontiac, Buick, Ford.

Hummingbird, disguised as one of them,
found shapes to vent his anger.
once more the dismal drum of bold Hui-chil-o-bos
shakes the hills
with the sound of conch and blaring horns.

the silver helmets roar and grind and screech
in mighty battle.

all around, with acrid smoke,
Mexico's blood spills out

and roadside shrines
mark the place of sacrifice.

**Of Bones**

I'm reading from a book as thick
and full of words as grandma's
family bible was when I was just
a tot of three or four and held
that tome upon my lap
to read the pictures front
to back at grandma's house
all warm and snug,
so very long ago

I'm reading now how, on this continent
we call our home from north to south,
the native people wrote their stories down
in folding books before the strangers came
to rape their land and burn the words
they could not understand because
the homes they came from weren't
as civilized and grand as these.

The strangers marvelled at the fields
of maize and orchards filled
with fruit and nuts and sweet berries
but scorned the sacred texts
they could not trust
because they knew not stars.

and so they scrambled gold
and slaves and brought
the spotted sickness into gleaming halls
and homes and temples and the people
fell as strangers took the land
we now call home.

# La Manzanilla

## Carmelita's Garden

Here on a sandy bank, above the pounding surf,
the ghost of little Carmelita, no more than five.
romps alone, beneath the stars.
Long past her time for bed,
she sings her spirited circle game:

Oh chepi, chepi, chepi, oh lero, lero le.
Oh chepi, chepi, chepi, oh lero, lero le.

She skips out past her tiny garden,
to join the weeds beyond.
No children come to play.
Only Mother Nature embraces her –
dogs, seagulls, horny lizards, scorpions.

Where someone has lit a fire to burn the trash,
she cheerily sings by the mausoleums --
plastic lilies, cracked vases,
faded wreaths, cement and wooden crosses,
and dusty tombs all covered by weeds.

Oh chepi, chepi, chepi, oh lero, lero le.
Oh chepi, chepi, chepi, oh lero, lero le.

**Footprints**

Upon this sunny mile,
footprints leave swirls in the sparkling sand
amidst sparkling mica – Aztec gold.
Before I turn to leave my prints anew,
the timeless tide has erased every trace.
My path is not marked for long.

**Street Sweeper**

why do you hand me a broom
when i ask for work?
did you ask what i can do?

my skin is dark.
so what?
my ancestors brought civilization to this world
when your ancestors slept in caves
and ate their fish raw.
yet you call me savage.

my skin is dark.
so what?

## Señora de la gota – Bead Lady

Weighed down with bags of beads,
hand-crafted rosaries, shell crucifixes,
trays of bracelets, necklaces, and earrings,
a colourful pedlar walks the strip.

Today, as every day, she approaches me,
insistent I see her wares.
I shake my head, "Non, gracias."
She persists. At last, I give in.

A set of tiny pearls catches my fancy.
I pay a sum, tiny for me, a day's wages for her.
Like crumbs dropped for hungry gulls, I'm marked.

Now, up and down the glistening mica beach,
every pedlar wants his share.
Husband, wife, father, mother, son, and daughter,
all lug their wares.

Before the sun-blaze on the sand,
the poor families walk in silhouette.
The children jump the waves, shriek to catch up.

All head for me.

## Sunset Shift at Café de Flores

Sunset flashes green on the purple sky
amidst orange, yellow, and golden clouds.
A kite glides the thermals;
swallows skitter, chasing gnats.

While strumming a twangy-mellow tune,
a guitarist speaks softly to us.
Tables are spread in Mexican array:
flickering candles, brilliant colours.

Suddenly the sky darkens.
Traffic and blaring megaphones overwhelm.
Here on the cafe rooftop,
life's cacophony dominates the night.

## Heartbreak Melody

Now, in the moonlight, on a sandy shore,
he sits and strums his heartbreak melody to the waves.
They don't care.

Last night he strolled beneath the moon
and sang eternal love.
He didn't know she planned to run away.

Now she's gone.
In the heat of the day,
her empty promises had melted away.

**Dog in the Heat of Day**

Is the dog dead?
He lies there in the dust,
beside the narrow sidewalk,
where a car could park
if he weren't there.

The dog was there yesterday
and the day before.
Does he guard his master's parking space?
Is he just old and tired?
Or is the dog dead?

**Dust**

In La Manzanilla, Mexico,
the scattered clouds are brilliant white and grey.
Grey, like the dust that seeps
through every nook and cranny,
covering tables, floors, windows, sidewalks, streets,
people's feet -- and me.

In the heat,
even the listless palm leaves are coated grey.
I lie back, gaze upwards at the brilliant, baby-blue sky,
and ponder the inevitable:
Soon it will be sunset. Soon the rains will come.
The dust will mix with water,
and wash the palm leaves, windows, and palappa roofs.
All will turn green;
all will sparkle in the humid summer.

When the dust returns,
the gringos will return.
They will sit in the sun by the sea
and drink their margaritas.
Gringos must like dust.

**Pelican**

A pelican skims the waves,
flaps up, skims again, belly-flops
onto the water, catches a fish, sideways.
A silver tail flaps from his mighty beak.

Again and again,
he flips the fish and drops it --
until he holds it headfirst.
Only then does he stretch his neck
and swallow it.

The pelican looks so clumsy.
Yet he catches a glittering fish.
In my own awkward efforts,
maybe there's hope for me after all.


**Drummer**

The boy loves his drum.
With his ratta-tatts, boom-booms,
he leads the band.
There's power in love.


**Adios**

Reluctant to say "adios,"
I pace the beach a final time.
Too soon I'll fly to snow and rain,
my sun-glow barely started.

Sand remains between our toes;
the pounding surf still lingers.
The friends I've made I'll meet again --
perhaps in other climates.

# Hawaii

## Moonscape

Out past the Kona Airport
on Hawaii's Big Island,
the world is being born.
Lava rock bears epitaphs,
messages of love;
white stones against black.


## Reading at the Beach

During ten glorious days of sun, sea, and sand,
in the shade where golden finches came to beg,
we read fresh pages of long-awaited novels.

Surviving a tsunami that almost was –
and temporary evacuation,
no one seemed to mind.


## Kahalu'u Beach

Blue-finned,
we glide warm currents
over pink coral.
Brilliant creatures dart and feed
beneath the blazing sun.

Butterfly fish and fantails, anglers and octopi,
tiny turkey fish and great sea turtles all un-shy,
among blue jack, zebras, needlefish and parrot fish.

Beyond the reef,
boogie-boarders and surfers
ride on monster waves
while humpback whales frolic
in their mating dance,
leaping and slapping not far from shore.

## Afternoon Beneath a Parasol

First afternoon beneath a parasol,
I hear the surf:
It pounds, swishes, and roars
on black lava rocks,
thunders into hidden caves.

Chatter of birds
and sun-kissed ladies lolling
in bright blues
and greens beneath
coconut palms
and scattered clouds.

Flesh
baked bronze and patchy scarlet,
the slow-cooking ladies
drink their mai-tais
through twisted straws
from white-rimmed tumblers.

Not a hat among them.

# Sunshine Coast

# of

# British Columbia

## Madeira Park Palette

Rainbows glisten through sprinkler spray
on a golf-course lawn,
ablaze in red carnations,
pink petunias and blue lobelia,
all blooming in the mist.
On the front porch, grandpa slumbers in his rocker,
softly snoring in the morning sun.
A Yellow Warbler greets me with her song.

Bright flags flutter,
reds and blues and white and gold
across a robin-egg sky.
Navy-blue awnings flap
over milk-white boats.
A fisherman in orange shirt
coils rope along the wharf.
Two mighty eagles drift aloft
while crows and seagulls
chase and tease the pair.

In the crystal dockside water,
beneath the mossy bank,
held firm by copper-skinned Arbutus,
strands of bulb-kelp float like massive bullwhips,
jellyfish flutter – translucent water butterflies,
above brown-green crab,
orange starfish, rockfish and prawns.

Kayak paddlers gracefully glide.
A sailboat trails a yellow dingy.
Two outboard motors growl
and a dog barks.
Happy children play on the pier.
On the hillside,
in speckled sun among the ferns,
I hear the forest breathing,
while snow-capped mountains
slip into the sea.

## A Day Cruise on the Eagle

From Egmont, cruising north, the inlet's calm
and we relax in sun and cooling breeze
to view the ponderous slopes with snowy peaks
and seals that raise their heads like massive slugs
on rocky islets, while we drift slowly by.

Black mussels and white-shelled oysters mark the tides
along the granite cliffs where manganese leaches down in
white blotches.
And on a stretch of mossy shore,
age-stained boom-sticks stand forlorn in piles
to wait for harvests in another time

Beyond the Malibu Rapids,
Mt. Albert casts his head above the clouds.
Skidder trails zigzag down mountain slopes
in lighter green of alder amidst the pines,
like brush strokes of frustration
on a canvas of bright sun and darker hues.

Above "Deserted Bay", fire-burned tips,
like silver spires, stand tall
among the virgin green of new-growth –
Western Hemlock and Red Cedar.

## Princess Louisa Inlet
### Shíshálh First Nations name "wiwelát"

When the Creator made swiwelát,
long before the mile-thick ice rolled down,
he thrust his mighty arms up through the mud
and flung the seed of forests to each side,
among the crags of granite and green stone.

No finger from the sky pronounced the deed,
though claps of thunder echoed hill to hill.
Then crowds of raven, crow and eagle came
to call the task well done and state their claim.

## A Boat Called "Eagle"

An eagle swoops and glides with grace.
But this misnamed bronco bucks and kicks and slaps
and spits and scolds her way
through pounding waves,
as she slams the voyage home.
Her skipper, Tim, holds the reins,
firmer than Roy Rogers of cowboy fame
(or Buck, were this the starship of my youth).

*\*Skipper Tim Rogers*

## Chatterbox Falls

At Chatterbox, the falls cascade
in silver ribbons on ice-scraped granite.
From peaks and slopes, last winter's snow
descends in streams to meet the bay.

Like mossy antlers on a rutting deer,
lichen-covered trees embrace the misty spray
as water cascades
to splash the wind-swept bay.

## Flying the Skookumchuck

Whether Eagle, Lion, or killer whale,
we trust her for her strength
and for her skipper's skill.
Like a bull through ripping tides,
she braves the Sechelt Rapids
at Skookumchuck –
the fastest tidal current anywhere.
Always, we feel secure.

## Egmont Bay

flash, flash, splish-splash;
kayak paddles dip and stroke.
saltwater sprays with wind and tide.

far beneath the loggers' slash
we can glide,
gently glide,
gently glide.

flash, flash, splish-splash;
kayak paddles dip and glide,
dip and glide.

sail boats come and go most haughty
diesel motors aptly hidden
towing dinghies, flags-a-flutter.

pier hands run when they are bidden
big bucks call;
they're not denied.

soon with full sail they will glide,
gently glide;
proudly glide,
easy masters of the tide.

other boats for other folks
rumble slowly out from dock-side.
those too old and those too young
still enjoy the summer fun.
summer plays in Egmont Bay.

# Cuba

## Varadero Beach

Long, sand-filled waves splash bubbly crests of foam
in stripes of frothy white on turquoise blue.
Fresh flown from wet and snowy realms,
I gaze in wonder at this paradise.

Slathered top to toe with oily salve,
I lie beneath a palm parasol
and sip piña coladas through a straw
and spy dark, sun-soaked beauties all around.

## AUTHOR PROFILE

Ben Nuttall-Smith taught Music, Theatre, Art, and Language until he retired in 1991. Ben is a member and was 1st Vice President of the Federation of British Columbia Writers, a member of the Canadian Authors' Association, Editorial Board member for the Canadian Poetry Association quarterly magazine Poemata and member of the Writers' Union of Canada.

Publications include a book of poetry - A Moment In Eternity (Silver Bow 2013), an historical novel – Blood, Feathers and Holy Men, (Libros Libertad 2011), an autobiographical novel, Secrets Kept / Secrets Told, (Libros Libertad 2012), a 3500 word illustrated children's book – Henry Hamster Esquire and a book of Haiku for children illustrated by Jan Albertin –Grandpa's Homestead.

Ben's poems and short stories have appeared in numerous anthologies and online publications including All That Uneasy Spring editor, Patrick Lane; Quills Canadian Poetry Magazine; Poemata Canadian Poetry Association; Royal City Poets", Silver Bow Publishing," Between Earth and Sky", Silver Bow Publishing, "Lucidity Journal of Verse", Bear House Publishing, Houston, Texas; Cyclamens and Swords online poetry magazine.

Ben was the winner of The Surrey Board of Trade Special Achievement Award 2011 for work as a writer and for service to the writing community

www.ingramcontent.com/pod-product-compliance
Lightning Source LLC
Chambersburg PA
CBHW070151080526